Please return this training resource to the Learning and Development Department by the date shown.

REF:

DATE BOOKED OUT	DATE TO BE RETURNED

Published by:
Management Pocketbooks Ltd
Laurel House, Station Approach, Alresford, Hants SO24 9JH, U.K.
Tel: +44 (0)1962 735573   Fax: +44 (0)1962 733637
Email: sales@pocketbook.co.uk
Website: www.pocketbook.co.uk

© John Townsend & Paul Donovan 1999 and 2009

First published in 1999. This edition published 2009, reprinted 2010, 2012, 2014.
ISBN: 978 1 906610 08 1

Ebook ISBN: 978 1 908284 05 1

British Library Cataloguing-in-Publication Data. A catalogue record for this book is available from the British Library.

Design, typesetting and graphics by **efex Ltd.**   Printed in U.K.

CONTENTS

4

1NTRODUCTION

INTRODUCTION

DEFINITION OF FACILITATION

Literally, facilitation means 'making things easy'.

In today's workplaces, facilitators make things easier by:

Using a range of skills and methods to bring the best out in people as they work to achieve results in interactive events.

Typically, facilitators are asked to help people to make decisions and achieve results in meetings, teambuilding sessions, problem-solving groups and training events.

TYPICAL FACILITATION SITUATIONS

- The HR Director asks you to form a focus group and come up with suggestions to make the organisation's compensation and benefits package more competitive

- Absenteeism is increasing and it's not just because of seasonal illnesses. Top management has asked you to investigate the causes and present some solutions

- The organisation's 'social responsibility' footprint is to be upgraded and you are to facilitate a session to find ways to raise money for local and/or national charities

- Staff training cannot be linked to bottom-line results. You are asked to organise a session with department heads..... has all that training money been wasted?

- Customer service complaints are increasing. You are asked to facilitate a session with supervisors and employees and to present an action plan to reduce them

- HR have commissioned you to help tackle the problem of increased turnover in the organisation and you are planning a session with department heads next week

NB See pages 48 to 53 for Facilitation Session Templates for these typical situations

THE FACILITATOR'S ROLE

- **Generalist and Specialist**
  - general knowledge of how organisations function and specialised knowledge of organisational diagrams and intervention processes.

- **Co-ordinator**
  - the link between the client and the group. The organiser of resources and expertise.

- **Neutral Observer**
  - belonging to no political coalition within an organisation and being seen as having no stake in any outcome.

  Adapted from Beer (1980)

Facilitators have to be able to cope with uncertainty, knowing that things may not turn out as predicted or hoped for. They must be able to use the power of their credibility to help people address issues. They need to be calm in times of emotion when others are stressed and confused.

Facilitators need to be able to empathise with people and listen well. They need to be able to support and counsel others who may be having a hard time in the session; to describe in understandable ways the processes and systems they are proposing; to mobilise energy in self and client; to surface difficult issues and help others to do so; to take themselves less seriously and more humorously.

PLANNING THE FACILITATION SESSION

THE 3 PHASES OF FACILITATION

To 'make things easy' for a group and help them solve a problem or brainstorm ideas, the facilitator needs neutrality, clarity of thinking and, above all, a process. In this pocketbook we propose a 3-phase facilitation process which we have found will fit most situations:

Phase 1: Before the actual session you need to identify, with the sponsor/client, the undesirable or unacceptable **current situation;** set an **objective** defining the **desired outcome** of the session and the **format** this will take (list/chart/report?).

Phase 2: Arrange a session (2-4 hours) with a group of 6-12* representative, qualified and/or knowledgeable people; present the situation and the objective; then use a tested method to identify the **issues/problems** associated with the current situation.

Phase 3: At the same or at a second session, identify possible **solutions** to these problems and draw up an **action plan** – who will do what and by when.

* See page 14 for more on group sizes.

PHASE 1: CURRENT SITUATION

Many problem-solving sessions fail and many objectives are not reached quite simply because the people involved never really defined... *'Where are we coming from?'*

Unless we know precisely where we are now, it's difficult to set a meaningful and measurable goal and, unless we can measure it, we can't manage it!

So, the very first step in planning a facilitation session, is to specify the current situation as precisely as possible. What is happening now that is unacceptable? What exactly is the situation that should be changed?

Gather as much information about the present state of affairs as you can in the time available. Ask yourself/ the client/ the sponsor to provide measurable data as to what is happening now, so that you can start to formulate a measurable objective to reach.

PHASE 1: SESSION OBJECTIVE

The next step in phase 1 is to define the **SMART** (specific; measurable; attainable; relevant; time-bound) objective and, in agreement with the sponsor/client, the format of the output expected. Given the current situation, what are we aiming to achieve, realistically speaking, in the session?

A very useful way to formulate a session objective is to start with:

'By the end of this session'.....and then use the future perfect tense to define what **will have** happened and what the output will look like.

Example:
By the end of this session we will have produced (on one flip chart page) a five point action plan on how to improve XYZ.

PHASE 2: IDENTIFYING ISSUES/PROBLEMS

ARRANGING THE SESSION

Meeting Room/Facilities:
The facilitation process we are recommending in this pocketbook is extremely interactive and 'hands-on' so you will need a large meeting room with plenty of flip charts, pinboards, whiteboards and wall space, for keeping important lists/decisions, etc in view. Running a session in a cramped boardroom space will not help creativity and openness.

Special Equipment:
Most information-gathering and solution-finding methods require participants to write suggestions on post-its or cards and stick them onto pre-prepared boards, so you'll need a good supply of these as well as different coloured markers. There are also two main suppliers of specialist equipment for facilitators, that you may find helpful:
www.neuland.ie and **www.metaplan.com**

PHASE 2: IDENTIFYING ISSUES/PROBLEMS

ARRANGING THE SESSION (CONT'D)

Participants:

The attendees at the session will be chosen according to their knowledge/qualifications in the area to be discussed – unless they are the 'real' team who have asked for your help.

The ideal group size is between 6 and 12. Of course it's possible to have a successful session with a larger or smaller group, but this size enables you to hear from everyone easily, break into sub-groups and share findings more easily than with a larger group. It also avoids the relative lack of synergy and 'buzz' from a smaller group. Remember to include any stakeholders who could block final decisions.

Find out as much as you can about the participants before the session (personalities, hierarchical level, vested interests, pet gripes, etc) so as to be prepared for possible conflicts, time wasting, soap box attempts and so on.

PHASE 2: IDENTIFYING ISSUES/PROBLEMS

PREPARING THE SESSION: SEQUENCE

Now that the objective for the session is clear, the room is arranged and the attendees invited, you'll need to prepare the process. How will you help the group get from the situation now to the objective you have agreed with the sponsor?

Here are the components of the session that you'll have to prepare in advance:

- An **intro** – why are we here?
- A **'focus' question** which will ask the group to engage with you on the importance/size/urgency of the problem
- A discussion of the **objective** for the session....is it realistic and acceptable?
- Some suggested ground rules for the session to avoid conflict/sidetracking/disturbances
- A **'discussion' question** to launch the session and identify the issues to be resolved
- An **information-gathering process** – to collect, sort and prioritise the information obtained in answer to the discussion question

The following pages explain each of these components in more detail.

(15)

PHASE 2: IDENTIFYING ISSUES/PROBLEMS

PREPARING THE SESSION: INTRODUCTION

It is important to plan how you will introduce the session.
Most of the participants will be busy people, who set a
value on every minute of their day. Show them from the
start that you're competent and organised and here
to help them.

Once an organisation gets used to
facilitators doing a professional
job there's no question as to
their credibility, but for the first
few sessions you may have to
establish yours....with subtlety.

PHASE 2: IDENTIFYING ISSUES/PROBLEMS

PREPARING THE SESSION: INTRODUCTION

How will you outline the reasons for the meeting? What do the sponsors want you to say about the current situation? What will you say about who you are and why you are running the session. Will you explain that you may not be an expert on **their** operation but that you are an expert on helping people solve problems?

Will all the participants know each other? If not… will you need to do any more 'positioning' before starting the session?

PHASE 2: IDENTIFYING ISSUES/PROBLEMS

PREPARING THE SESSION: FOCUS QUESTION

People rarely give their energy to something without a strong 'felt need', ie they understand that something **needs** doing and they **want** to do it. Getting in touch with this 'felt need' isn't always spontaneous, so this is a crucial part of the facilitator's work.

A powerful way to start any facilitation session – after the brief introduction – is to ask participants to 'focus' by giving a simple 'spot check' evaluation. This can be done on a flip chart outlining how they feel about the current situation relative to the objective. As the facilitator you will also need to have planned a 'Discussion Question' – used later to gather more detail (see page 23). Planning ahead ensures that the focus question does just that, focus on the underlying issue. Here are some examples of how a challenging focus question might be phrased:

● How important do you think it is to improve *xyz*?

● How comfortable are you with situation *abc*?

● To what extent is *xyz* causing friction in your department?

● On the road to perfect *abc,* where are we now?

● To what degree do you believe that absenteeism is a serious problem here?

PHASE 2: IDENTIFYING ISSUES/PROBLEMS

PREPARING THE SESSION: FOCUS QUESTION (CONT'D)

The most effective focus questions are ones which ask participants to give their opinions on a scale rather than as a yes or no. This is a **one-dimensional question** and can be done by pre-preparing a flip chart page, writing out the question and providing a scale from low to high. Ask participants to give their opinion or commitment by sticking an adhesive dot onto the scale at the appropriate place (or making a cross with a board marker).

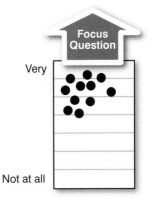

PHASE 2: IDENTIFYING ISSUES/PROBLEMS
PREPARING THE SESSION: FOCUS QUESTION (CONT'D)

You can also try **two-dimensional focus questions** by drawing a two axis graph and asking participants to answer two related questions by plotting their answer with one dot or a cross where their two scores meet.

Focus Question 1: How important are effective meetings to the success of our team?

Focus Question 2: On the road to meetings excellence where are we now?

A good focus question will allow you to discuss extreme ratings with the participants. Those whose views differ greatly from the rest of the group have the option of leaving the meeting or, despite their views, staying and helping the process.

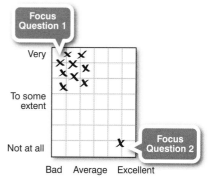

PLANNING THE FACILITATION SESSION

PHASE 2: IDENTIFYING ISSUES/PROBLEMS

PREPARING THE SESSION: OBJECTIVE

At this stage, you've already planned an objective for the session with the sponsor/client or have a pretty good idea of what **you** want to achieve with the group. Now you need to think ahead to the session itself and ask:

- How will I present the objective to the participants?
- To what extent is the objective up for discussion?
- Are you, or the sponsor/client, ready to modify it if the group have good arguments to do so?
- If they do want modifications, will I have to go back to the sponsor/client before proceeding?

Clarify these questions with all involved before going into the session and prepare any visual aids or handouts you will need.

PHASE 2: IDENTIFYING ISSUES/PROBLEMS
PREPARING THE SESSION: GROUND RULES

Having planned a good focus question you need to agree some ground rules with the group. These are essential for running a smooth facilitation session, especially when they are suggested by or agreed by the participants. Discussion may well get heated once problems and possible solutions start to fly. After all, you are there **because** there are issues to be resolved.

When a few ground rules concerning participant behaviour, process clarification, time limits, individual participation, interruptions, etc are set and agreed, you, as the facilitator, won't have to 'control' the session or be authoritative or disciplinary. If needed, you can refer the group back to **their** rules and ask them how any incident should be handled.

PHASE 2: IDENTIFYING ISSUES/PROBLEMS

PREPARING THE SESSION: DISCUSSION QUESTION

It is vital to formulate the 'discussion' question in a way that ensures the discussion is centred on moving from the current situation to the objective and not sidetracked. Unless you are clearly in a simple brainstorming situation, eg *'We need 10 ideas on possible new products',* a discussion question should ask for details of the problem and not solutions. For this reason it should be phrased negatively! Examples:

- **What's hindering our teamwork?**
- **What's wrong with our meetings?**
- **Why are so many people leaving the organisation?**
- **Why is training not having an impact on the organisation's results?**

If the discussion question is phrased positively ('How can we improve...? What can we do to increase...?') the group will look for solutions without having explored all the problems and they might miss something vital!

NB You need to plan this question **before** formulating the opening focus question, just to be sure that the focus question concentrates on the issues the discussion question will raise.

PHASE 2: IDENTIFYING ISSUES/PROBLEMS

PREPARING THE SESSION: INFORMATION GATHERING

Having asked the discussion question you will hopefully be inundated with replies, but how are you going to capture them, and organise the gathering of all this information?

Years ago facilitators, however skilled, would encourage participants to give their input and laboriously record all contributions on a sequential list on a flip chart. Since the advent of pinboards, post-its and other 'metaplanning' facilitation techniques, information gathering has become quicker and tighter, and more manageable.

PHASE 2: IDENTIFYING ISSUES/PROBLEMS

PREPARING THE SESSION: INFORMATION GATHERING

Participants (separately or in pairs or trios) are given 5-10 minutes to write down their ideas on cards or post-its and stick them onto large boards (see the 'Talking Wall' on page 98). This means that everybody gets to give their ideas – even the shy ones who tended to get 'talked over' in the old days.

It's probably best to ask people to stick their answers to the discussion question up on the board organically (not in columns or clusters yet). Or, to save time, you could suggest they stick their suggestions into pre-prepared columns on a board, to help the categorisation process.

PLANNING THE FACILITATION SESSION

PHASE 2: IDENTIFYING ISSUES/PROBLEMS
PREPARING THE SESSION: CATEGORISING & PRIORITISING

The next step is to sort the information just gathered. You will have a lot of cards – many of them overlapping or duplicating each other (from separate pairs or trios) and you'll need to 'chunk' them into pieces you can work with. For this you will need to think about how you will cluster and categorise the cards.

- The simplest way is to ask the group to help you eliminate duplicates (never take duplicates off the board without the writers' permission!) and then start clustering groups of cards by similarity. You can either get the group to pronounce on each card as to whether it goes in an existing or a new category, or get them to do it in a kind of shoulder-rubbing free-for-all. You'll probably want to put new HEADING cards onto each of the clusters or columns

- Next, you need the group to prioritise the categories of issues/problems you have produced. The 'Five Vote Method' works well for this. Each participant gets five votes to distribute to the various category headings in any way they see fit

PHASE 3: FINDING SOLUTIONS/ACTION PLAN

PREPARING THE SESSION: METHODOLOGY

We have separated the solution finding and action planning phase of the facilitation process into phase 3 because you may not wish (or even be able) to run this session immediately following phase 2: problems/issues. You may decide to run this phase of the facilitation a week or so later.

In the solution-finding techniques chapter later in the book there are 10 different methods which you can use at this stage of your facilitation – from the classic 'Brainstorming' to the not so classic 'Eureka'. Each is a tried and tested way of helping a group to come up with solutions to problems.

PHASE 3: FINDING SOLUTIONS/ACTION PLAN
PREPARING THE SESSION: METHODOLOGY (CONT'D)

Whichever method you decide to use, it's probably a good idea to break the participants into smaller groups and ask them to work on solutions/ideas to be presented to the whole group later.

Example:
'Causes and Solutions' and 'Time Beam' are good, standard, no-risk methods for down-to-earth issues, whereas 'Eureka', and 'This Time Next Year' would be applicable to problem-solving sessions where the group is looking for creative solutions and is willing to operate outside the box.

Instead of getting groups to present their solutions verbally, try a 'Vernissage' where each group creates a pinboard, whiteboard or flip chart of ideas which is then visited by the other groups like the 'vernissage' (private viewing) at an art gallery (full explanation on page 99).

PHASE 3: FINDING SOLUTIONS/ACTION PLAN

PREPARING THE SESSION: ACTION PLAN

A facilitation session is only as good as its action plan! The road to
a waste of time and money is paved with the good intentions
expressed at the end of many a meeting!
Quite simply, now's the time for *you* to plan how you
will help the group make *their* plan!

PHASE 3: FINDING SOLUTIONS/ACTION PLAN

PREPARING THE SESSION: ACTION PLAN (CONT'D)

Before finalising the action plan you may want to help the group to do a 'reality test' on one or other of the great solutions they have come up with. 'Force Field Analysis' and 'Must Have/Nice To Have' are techniques for doing just that.

Remember the format you agreed for the output of the session, and prepare how to lead the 'action planning discussion' toward recording the output in that format.

Above all, the key question will always be:

WHO will do WHAT and by WHEN?

CASE STUDY

Example of a 3-phase
facilitation session

CASE STUDY

PHASE 1: CURRENT SITUATION

Congratulations! You are the facilitator in our case study described in this chapter, and you have just successfully concluded the third and final phase of a facilitation process to help resolve a particular issue. Read on to discover how you did it!

The director of one of your organisation's key departments asked for help in improving the weekly staff meetings. These are attended by six direct line reports and four staff managers, who take it in turns to chair the meetings.

At the first discussion concerning the 'current situation', you learned from the director that she had been hearing complaints about these meetings from the attendees. Some complaints were specific (poor chairing skills, no agenda) and some more general (time wasting, no focus).

She thought that a neutral, outside facilitator could arrange a special session to help the team have a good look at these issues and come up with some ideas on how to improve the quality and output of their weekly meetings.

PHASE 1: SESSION OBJECTIVE

To help the director formulate a measurable (SMART) objective for the session you asked: *'What will you accept as evidence that this facilitated session has been a success?'* After discussing a few possible outcomes and pieces of evidence, you both agreed that the objective you would propose to the team would be:

By the end of this session we will have produced (on one flip chart page) a five point action plan on how to improve our (weekly) meetings.

You asked for information about the attendees' record of participation in previous meetings and underlined the importance of the whole team being at the session (so nobody could block any of the proposed action plans later). The director preferred not to be at the session, so people could speak freely, but agreed the whole team should attend. You then scheduled the session for the following week, ie this morning at 09:00!

PHASE 2: IDENTIFYING ISSUES/PROBLEMS
ARRANGING THE SESSION

Meeting Room/Facilities:

A medium size conference room was booked for this morning's session with the following equipment: four flip charts; four pinboards. Because of the information-gathering and solution-finding methods you were planning on using, you also ordered four post-it note blocks and 10 black markers plus a selection of coloured marker pens. You anticipated breaking the team into three sub groups and needed one flip chart and pinboard for your own visuals. Before the session you prepared the flip charts with the focus question and objectives, as well as the 'prioritisation pinboard' (see pages 36 and 44).

Participants:

Before everyone arrived at this morning's session you looked back at the notes you had made during your interview with the director and, from your own knowledge of some of the more outspoken members of the team, decided that you would be proposing a couple of clear 'behavioural' ground rules for the session – to allow everyone else to have their say and to avoid getting bogged down in 'turf' issues.

PHASE 2: IDENTIFYING ISSUES/PROBLEMS
INTRODUCING THE SESSION: YOUR NOTES

Explain: Who am I? Introduce myself to those who don't know me.

Explain: Why am I here? 'The director has heard your remarks concerning the effectiveness of your weekly meetings and asked for my help'.

Explain why the director is not here.

Give time limit for meeting: 8.30 - 12.00 with 15 minute break at 10.00.

Explain that I have a step by step process which will allow them to discuss the extent to which they agree with the director, that there is a problem with the meetings, and, if so, come up with some solutions (NB: probably use 'causes and solutions' methods for solution-finding phase).

Ask for questions on the introduction.

The introduction went well with only a couple of murmurings about 'meetings about meetings' and 'hope it's better than the usual' but, all in all, a relatively good humoured and co-operative start.

(35)

CASE STUDY

PHASE 2: IDENTIFYING ISSUES/PROBLEMS
THE FOCUS QUESTION

After your interview with the director you had decided on the discussion question you would ask the team: *'What's wrong with our meetings?'* and then came up with the following focus question which you hoped would get each person to show you and the group how bad they thought the present meetings are: *'On the road to meetings excellence, where are we now?'*

You wrote the questions on a flip chart and asked the team to give their rating by sticking a self-adhesive dot somewhere along the road from 'terrible meetings' to 'excellent meetings'.

PHASE 2: IDENTIFYING ISSUES/PROBLEMS

THE FOCUS QUESTION

Eight dots were placed between 'terrible' and 'average', one slightly above 'average' and one near the 'excellent' rating. Remaining open and neutral, you asked the two 'odd ones out' to comment on their ratings. It became clear that they thought that meetings were always terrible and that theirs were no worse (and sometimes better) than the average. You realised that they wanted to make a point in public. You asked if they felt it was worth staying in the session and helping the team to tease out the problems and find some possible solutions to improving the meetings, and they readily agreed.

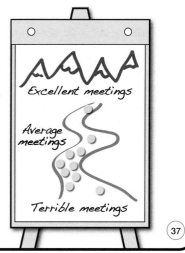

PHASE 2: IDENTIFYING ISSUES/PROBLEMS

AGREEING ON THE OBJECTIVE

With the team focused on the issue, you introduced the proposed objective on a flip chart:

By the end of this session we will have produced (on one flip chart page) a five point action plan on how to improve our (weekly) meetings.

You asked for agreement and comments. There were some comments on the specificity of the objective ('Why five points…what if we only have three…?') which you handled non-defensively and then the team agreed to try and go for it.

PHASE 2: IDENTIFYING ISSUES/PROBLEMS
GROUND RULES

In preparation for conflicting opinions and ideas later, it was time to set some ground rules. You explained that during the session they would be asked to work in pairs and come up with issues on cards/post-its. Then in three larger groups they would explore the causes of the problems and brainstorm solutions.

To ensure that any disagreements would be positive and not destructive you proposed:

- Be hard on the problems but not on the people

- Everyone must participate with ideas and solutions – taking turns to contribute

- Write clearly on cards in large capital letters – 10 words max – to ensure legibility

CASE STUDY

PHASE 2: IDENTIFYING ISSUES/PROBLEMS
GROUND RULES (CONT'D)

Ground rules suggested by the group were:

- Appoint a timekeeper to keep track of the time frames set by the facilitator, and a 'watchdog' who would be in charge of signalling any rule breaking

- Switch off all mobile phones

- No interrupting when someone is giving their ideas

You then summarised these rules in KEY WORDS on a flip chart sheet and stuck them on the front wall of the meeting room.

PHASE 2: IDENTIFYING ISSUES/PROBLEMS
DISCUSSION QUESTION/INFORMATION GATHERING

As planned you then launched into the discussion question:

What's wrong with our meetings?

- The team broke into five pairs to write as many criticisms as possible of the way their meetings were organised/run. This 'negativity' was an important part of the process because, unless they looked at all the possible problems, they might miss something vital to work on

- Each pair was given seven minutes to brainstorm *'what's wrong'* before sticking their ideas onto the pre-prepared board with the discussion question written at the top

PHASE 2: IDENTIFYING ISSUES/PROBLEMS
CLUSTERING & CATEGORISING

There were a lot of stickies up on the board! Several mentioned 'no agenda' and 'no follow-up' but there were also a lot which said things like 'bad chairing skills' or 'disruptive participants'. Now it was time to sort the information into meaningful and useful chunks.

The clustering and categorising method used was: get the whole group up at the board and ask THEM to sort the cards into clusters of similarity. You were then able to intervene *to ask questions like…. 'Are we sure that abc doesn't fit with xyz?' and 'Would it be possible to start a new cluster with this one?'*.

PHASE 2: IDENTIFYING ISSUES/PROBLEMS
CLUSTERING & CATEGORISING (CONT'D)

Once a cluster was finalised and everyone agreed it didn't overlap with other clusters, the group gave it a heading name (phrased as a problem) so as to make it a problem category. Some of the heading names they came up with were:

- **Lack of agenda**
- **Inappropriate meeting behaviour**
- **No action plan or follow up**
- **Inadequate chairing**
- **Important attendees missing**

43

PHASE 2: IDENTIFYING ISSUES/PROBLEMS
PRIORITISING

The problem category headings were then transferred from the 'clustered board' to the 'prioritisation board' – the idea being to come up with the three most urgent problems to work on as a group.

The board was divided into five columns: **problem category** (for the transferred cards), **teams, votes, score** and **rank.**

Each participant had five adhesive dots and used them to vote for those problem categories that they felt needed priority attention – in any way they saw fit (five on one problem or four on one and one on another, three on one and two on another, etc). You counted the scores and recorded them in the 'score' column and then ranked the top three in the 'rank' column. The participants then wrote their names on post-it notes and put their names in the 'teams' column against the top three issues they most wanted to work on. This gave three groups for phase 3 of the process.

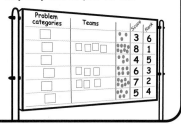

CASE STUDY

PHASE 3: FINDING SOLUTIONS/ACTION PLAN

CAUSES & SOLUTIONS

After a coffee break you moved into the final part of the session, phase 3 – finding solutions and making an action plan. The planned **causes and solutions** method* was explained to the three groups.

The groups had 30 minutes to come up with at least three root causes for their chosen problem category (looking for deep causes rather than superficial ones) and find at least three solutions.

During the creative brainstorming session there were a couple of heated discussions and raised voices in one group, but having intervened and asked the team how the exchanges fitted with the ground rules, the 'auto-correction' was almost immediate!

After 30 minutes you called time and organised a vernissage* of the three teams' boards. During the 'gallery visit' several ideas were awarded hearts and these were shortlisted for the final action plan.

* You'll meet both these methods in the chapter 'Solution Finding Techniques'.

CASE STUDY

PHASE 3: FINDING SOLUTIONS/ACTION PLAN

ACTION PLAN

For this final and satisfying step you reminded the group of the objective agreed upon at the start, namely to produce a flip chart with a five point action plan.

The vernissage had produced four items with hearts next to them, indicating that the group had considered these ideas to be their favourites. They were:

1. Standard meeting ground rules to be written and applied at all meetings, including timekeeper/watchdog to be appointed.
2. Prior written agenda to be issued.
3. Hand written minutes to be taken and copied for everyone before they leave.
4. Meetings to be re-scheduled when key players were not able to attend.

After checking with the group that these four points should be retained, a show of hands indicated that the fifth point, chosen from the remaining ideas on the board, should be 'meeting skills training' for them all! After brainstorming allocation of the work involved, a deadline was set for each step. The result – on one sheet – 'WHO will do WHAT by WHEN!' A member of the team agreed to present the action plan to the boss tomorrow. Fingers crossed!

FACILITATION SESSION TEMPLATES

Examples of key elements of the 3-phase process
for six typical facilitation sessions

EXAMPLE 1: CUSTOMER COMPLAINTS

Situation: Customer service complaints are increasing, though the cause is not clear. You have been asked to facilitate a focus group of supervisors and employees from different departments and to present an action plan on how to reduce these complaints.

Objective: By the end of this meeting to have identified the main causes of customer dissatisfaction and have produced an action plan on at least five ways to eliminate complaints.

Focus Question: On the road to perfect customer service where are we now? (Draw a 'road' on the flip chart from 'really bad' to 'perfect'. Provide dots/markers to participants.)

Discussion Question: Which customer interfaces or procedures (or lack of them) are causing complaints?

Process:
- Collect problems on stickies
- Cluster, name categories, prioritise
- Run a 'Causes/Solutions' exercise with 2-3 groups (see page 89)
- Vernissage results (see page 99)
- Prioritise solutions and, if necessary, test for feasibility with 'Force Field Analysis' (see page 100)
- Draw up action plan

EXAMPLE 2: TRAINING TRANSFER

Situation: The boss is worried that training money is being wasted. When she asked department heads about the impact of training on their team's performance, none of them could show any link between the training their people had received and bottom line results. You are to investigate by facilitating a session with all her direct reports.

Objective: To have identified ways in which we can improve, measurably, the management of training transfer.

Focus Question: 1.To what extent do you think that training **should** improve performance? Or 2. Is **presently** leading to...(draw two arrows on flip, from 'Not at all' to 'always'. Give dots/ markers.)

Discussion Question: Why does so much of the training we do seem to have so little effect on performance improvement?

Process:
- Pairs/trios brainstorm reasons on stickies
- Cluster, name categories, prioritise
- Run a 'Causes/Solutions' exercise with 2-3 groups
- Vernissage results with hearts for preferred solutions
- If necessary, test for feasibility with 'Force Field Analysis'
- Draw up action plan

EXAMPLE 3: RAISING MONEY FOR CHARITY

Situation: The CEO has decided to upgrade the 'social responsibility footprint' of your organisation. You are to facilitate a session with a representative group of employees to find ways in which you could raise money for local and/or national charities.

Objective: By the end of this meeting we will have 5-10 feasible ideas to present to the CEO on how we could raise money and for which local/national charities.

Focus Question: How willing are you to help us help others? (Draw smiley faces on flip, from 'happy' to 'sad' and give dots/markers.)

Discussion Question: 1. Which charities should we be helping? 2. What ideas have you on how we could raise money?

Process:
- Ask trios to brainstorm charities they think should be supported. Vote for preferred, keep top three
- Break into three groups (one for each selected charity) and brainstorm fund-raising ideas. Ask groups to vote and select top three ideas
- Vernissage each group's three ideas and consolidate onto one board to be presented to the CEO

EXAMPLE 4: STAFF TURNOVER

Situation: The HR Director has asked you to help him tackle the problem of increasing staff turnover. Year to date turnover is 12% versus 6.5% last year. Other companies in your region are averaging 7%. You are to facilitate a meeting of department heads.

Objective: By the end of this meeting to have identified 3-10 causes of the recent increase in staff turnover.

Focus Question: Two dimensions: a) To what degree do you believe that turnover is a serious problem in our organisation? b)...that we should identify what's causing it? ('very much/not at all?')

Discussion Question: Why do you think people are leaving this organisation?

Process:
- Ask trios to brainstorm reasons on stickies
- Cluster, name categories, prioritise
- Draw up final, ranked list of reasons
- Schedule next 'search for solutions' meeting

EXAMPLE 5: REWARD SYSTEM

Situation: A recent employee attitude survey shows half of the respondents are dissatisfied with the organisation's reward system. You are to put together a focus group and come up with some suggestions on how to make compensation and benefits more competitive.

Objective: By the end of this meeting to have identified 3-5 ways in which we can 'revamp' our organisation's reward system.

Focus Question: How urgent do you think it is to review our reward system? (Draw an arrow on a flip chart from 'not urgent' to 'very urgent'. Give dots or markers.)

Discussion Question: What's wrong with the way we reward our people?

Process:
- Ask pairs to brainstorm problems on stickies
- Cluster, name categories, prioritise
- Use any appropriate solution-finding technique depending on the group (see page 87 onwards)
- Vernissage solutions
- Vote on top five and draw up action plan

EXAMPLE 6: ABSENTEEISM

Situation: Absenteeism in your organisation is going up – and it's not just because of seasonal illness. The figures are frightening: last 12 months = 9.6%; previous 12 months = 4%; year before = 3%; local average = 3.2%. You are asked to assemble a small team to investigate the causes and suggest some solutions.

Objective: By the end of this meeting to have an action plan on how to reduce absenteeism by x% (To be completed after the Focus Question has been answered by the group).

Focus Question: To what degree do you believe we can influence absenteeism? (Draw a line on a flip chart, from 'very much' to 'not at all'. Give dots or markers.)

Discussion Question: Why do you think absenteeism is so high – and increasing?

Process:
- Ask pairs to brainstorm reasons on stickies
- Cluster, name categories, prioritise
- Run a 'This Time Next Year' solution-finding exercise (see page 91)
- Vernissage solutions
- Prioritise and test solutions for feasibility with 'Force Field Analysis'
- Draw up final action plan

NOTES

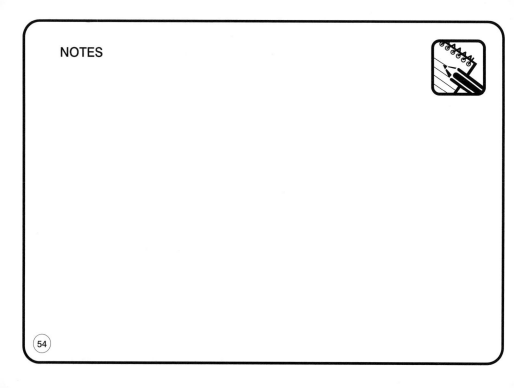

Facilitation methods

THE FACILITRAINING RAINBOW

The two key ingredients in any facilitation/training intervention are:
1. How much interaction does the facilitator have with participants?
2. How much does the facilitator contribute to the content/outcome of the session?
All 'facilitraining' interventions are a mixture of these two ingredients.

Here is a way of deciding which method to use and when. Using the criteria on the chart under the rainbow (and any others you want to add) simply score the session on the billiard-type sliding scales.

Examples:

- How much time will you have for the session? The less time available, the more likely you are to have to contribute more yourself and interact less with participants

- What is participants' present knowledge of the subject? The more they know the more you just facilitate the process

- What do participants expect from the session – to be told what to do, to discuss or to decide? Depending on the organisational/geographical culture you may start by presenting and only move to process monitoring later in the session

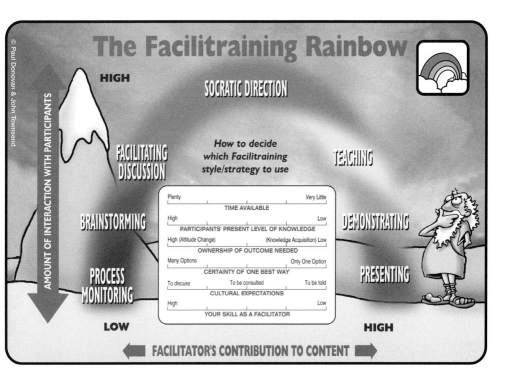

PROCESS MONITORING

(Low interaction/low contribution)

As the 'guardian of the process', the facilitator makes no personal contribution to the content of the discussion but occasionally regulates the flow of participants' contributions, according to a previously agreed set of process rules.

FACILITATION METHODS

BRAINSTORMING

(Low to medium interaction/low contribution)

Here the facilitator 'conducts' a classic brainstorming session – interacting with participants only to encourage them to give their ideas, but hardly ever evaluating or adding ideas.

FACILITATING DISCUSSION

(Medium to high interaction/low to medium contribution)

When using this style the facilitator interacts quite often with participants to invite opinions, control the process and give own opinions (if only to provoke more discussion).

FACILITATING DISCUSSION

SOCRATIC DIRECTION

(High interaction/medium to high contribution)

This is the method pioneered by Socrates whereby the facilitator asks questions and then reformulates the answers as necessary to lead participants to a desired learning outcome. The rainbow provides for a wide range of leading strategies – from relatively open to relatively closed.

The common element in all Socratic strategies is the high amount of interaction. It is based on the premise that people don't argue with their own data, even when it is massaged and channelled towards a 'hidden' learning outcome – as long as the 'facipulation' is done professionally and sincerely.

FACILITATION METHODS

TEACHING

(Medium to high interaction/medium to high contribution)

When, in the classic teaching mode, the facilitator provides structured learning experiences and guides participants towards pre-determined learning objectives. He or she, nevertheless, allows some latitude for interpretation at an individual level.

DEMONSTRATING

(Medium to low interaction/high contribution)

Not as 'one-way' as lecturing, demonstration involves interaction with participants, in as much as they are asked to try out in some way what has been presented.

PRESENTING

(Low interaction/high contribution)

The classical and often vital style needed to put across information.

However, as competition from the multimedia environment grows, trainers need to perform at an increasingly professional pitch to stop being 'zapped', or tuned out, by participants!

SESSION SKILLS

SETTING THE SCENE

The first skill needed by a facilitator in any situation is that of making people feel that they are welcome and in good hands. You demonstrate this skill when you:

- Engage in useful small talk
- Build rapport by linking to participants' experiences
- Describe objectives in a way that appeals to everyone
- Establish credibility by connecting to participants' concerns/jargon, etc

Yo!

SESSION SKILLS

STIMULATING INTEREST & CURIOSITY

Facilitation means making it easy for people to discuss and decide. They will only discuss and decide if they are motivated to do so. This means that a good facilitator will:

● Phrase discussion and focus questions that are inviting
  (see pages 18 to 20 and 23)

● Supply attractive processes with which to analyse and solve problems
  (see pages 88 to 98)

VALORISING PARTICIPANTS

In all participant-led facilitation sessions a key skill is to make the attendees all feel **valued**. This is what we mean by 'valorise'.

In order to accomplish this, the facilitator must:

- Adopt 'unconditional positive regard' for all participants – it's **their** session after all
- Boost quieter individuals' confidence by encouraging their contributions
- Build on people's suggestions
- Banter with extroverts

SEEKING CONSENSUS

Consensus is not when everyone agrees but when they agree to agree! In order to help a group reach consensus, the professional facilitator will:

- Identify points of agreement
- Reformulate contributions to highlight common ideas
- Explore people's objectives
- Encourage people to build on others' ideas
- Test false consensus due to conformity (is agreement real?)
- Test consensus for relevance to objective
- Test consensus for underlying motivation (is agreement biased in any way?)

PROVOKING USEFUL CONTROVERSY

Philosophers refer to 'Thesis/Antithesis/Synthesis'. Useful controversy means looking at both sides of a problem before deciding what to do. Professional facilitators do this when they:

- Phrase challenging questions (see page 76)
- Supply 'reframing' and/or creative solution-finding techniques (see pages 88 to 98)

They will also be skilled at dealing with the inevitable conflict which controversy brings and will:

- Reassert agreed ground rules on interpersonal behaviour
- Help the group 'be tough on the problem but not on the people'

DISTINGUISHING BETWEEN ESSENTIAL & NON-ESSENTIAL CONTRIBUTIONS

This is one of the most important and yet the most difficult facilitation skills. It's obviously easier when the facilitator knows the participants and their problem inside out. However, this is often not the case. In fact, it's more often the opposite. The facilitator is called in precisely because he or she does not know the content/subject matter and can, therefore, remain neutral. So we must:

- Constantly relate contributions to session objectives

- Monitor participants' body language for significant reactions to contributions and to people (What do **they** seem to think is essential? Whom do **they** seem to take most seriously during discussions?)

- Monitor group behaviour for clues to organisational pressure on decisions (What do **they** seem to think is important for the organisation? Whom do they listen to/agree with most?)

RECOGNISING COMMONALITIES, THEMES & TRENDS

The whole idea of facilitation is to build on common ground, to build consensus, to build decisions. A key skill for this is to recognise what **is** common ground. Experience is the best teacher here so, when in doubt as to whether there is commonality:

- Explore people's intentions and key concerns by asking for clarification to help your growing hypotheses
- Listen for frequently used words and phrases from different people which imply that consensus is building (or not!)

REVITALISING THE GROUP

From time to time even the best facilitated sessions run out of steam. A good facilitator will recognise these dips instantly and react quickly to:

- Supply energisers
- Refocus on the value of the discussion
- Bring people into the discussion who seem to be drifting
- Engage people who had useful contributions earlier but maybe now think they have nothing to add

ORIENTING THE GROUP TO ACTION

Too many facilitation sessions end when everyone 'feels good' rather than when a decision has been made. Since the objective of any facilitation session is to reach an objective, the facilitator will:

- Brainstorm action options
- Supply useful prioritisation techniques
- Supply decision-making methods
- Help the group to phrase decisions
- Assist in allocating tasks and responsibilities

Summarising

At the end of every session a good facilitator will:

- Recap the chronology of the session
- Highlight the key consensus items
- Reiterate the action plan

INTERPERSONAL SKILLS

QUESTIONING

The ability to ask good questions is vital to the success of a facilitator. But the information you get is only as good as the questions you ask.

Closed questions (those which only have one answer)
Sometimes it's necessary to collect concrete information from a group and a good closed questioning technique will help you do this efficiently. **'Who, what, when, where?'** questions will get you tight information and, if you add words like 'specifically?' and 'exactly?' to your question, you'll help people to be even more precise.

Open questions (those which have many answers)
At all stages of a facilitation, open questions ensure open discussions.

Examples:
'Tell me **about**...'
'**How** do you feel when...?'
'**Why** do you think this happened?'
'**What** would you do if...'

LISTENING

As a facilitator, in order to listen you have to talk!

That is, you have to show you're listening. And the way to show you're listening is to ask reflective questions or 'reformulate' what you think you heard someone saying. This **active** listening is vital to the smooth running of any facilitation process. It's probably **the** key skill for any facilitator.

Good listening means concentrating hard on the whole message from someone:

- Watching their body language for congruence with the message they're giving
- Listening to the kinds of words they're using; trying to understand where they're coming from as they speak
- Checking growing hypotheses about how what they're saying fits with the discussion so far
- Resisting temptation to double guess without reflecting back what you think you're hearing

GIVING FEEDBACK 1

Giving feedback can be an important part of some facilitation sessions – especially those contained within a training programme.

There is no doubt that people improve and grow most when they receive sincere feedback on what they do well, and are given constructive help to find ways of overcoming barriers to their effectiveness.

Whenever you are asked to facilitate giving feedback to a group or to individuals, help them to think through these three questions:

1. **What did you do well?**
2. **What could you have done even better?**
3. **What prevented you from doing even better; what's the plan to do even better in the future?**

INTERPERSONAL SKILLS

GIVING FEEDBACK 2
THE WIZARD OF OZ FACTOR

Like the Wizard of Oz who conferred his gifts upon the Tin Man, the Lion and the Scarecrow, we should affirm people into greatness! Often, because of our lack of line authority, we underestimate what a powerful force for personal growth we can be.

If we can show people a picture of themselves as successful and competent, then they have a much greater chance of becoming successful and competent than if we confirm their present negative self-image. Let's concentrate on the things they have done well, estimate their potential in that area, and then give feedback to them as if they have already achieved success.

- Build on their strengths
- Give them heart and courage; make them feel intelligent and powerful
- Show them how to feel ten feet tall and then they will be ready to take to the yellow brick road!

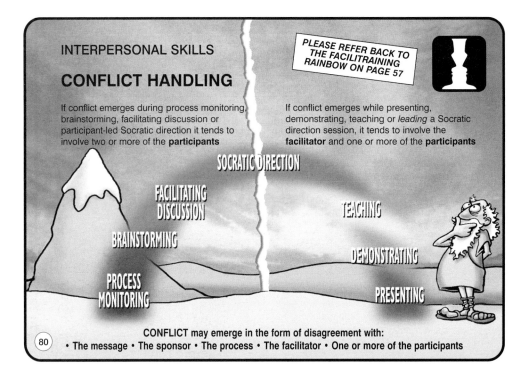

INTERPERSONAL SKILLS

CONFLICT HANDLING

PLEASE REFER BACK TO THE FACILITRAINING RAINBOW ON PAGE 57

If conflict emerges during process monitoring, brainstorming, facilitating discussion or participant-led Socratic direction it tends to involve two or more of the **participants**

If conflict emerges while presenting, demonstrating, teaching or *leading* a Socratic direction session, it tends to involve the **facilitator** and one or more of the **participants**

SOCRATIC DIRECTION

FACILITATING DISCUSSION

TEACHING

BRAINSTORMING

DEMONSTRATING

PROCESS MONITORING

PRESENTING

CONFLICT may emerge in the form of disagreement with:
• The message • The sponsor • The process • The facilitator • One or more of the participants

CONFLICT HANDLING WHEN PRESENTING

When a participant raises objections or 'heckles':

AFFIRM your position.
Restate your case.
Draw on new arguments to convince.

AVOID
Ignore the interruption.
Say you will handle questions later.
Ask for questioners to 'park' their
objections on a board.

INTERPERSONAL SKILLS

CONFLICT HANDLING WHEN DEMONSTRATING

When a participant raises objections or disagrees:

POSTPONE
Ask them to hold their thoughts until after the demo.

DEBATE
Enter a brief discussion to argue your point.
Support with examples.
Introduce new elements into the demo.

DEMONSTRATING

CONFLICT HANDLING WHEN TEACHING

When a participant raises objections or disagrees:

AGREE on minor points and accommodate their views in your teaching.

DISCUSS briefly the merits of the objection but reaffirm your position.

SHELVE items causing conflict until later.

CONFLICT HANDLING WHEN IN SOCRATIC DIRECTION

When a participant raises objections or disagrees:

REFLECT/DEFLECT

Reflect back what you think you heard.
Deflect to others for their views.

QUESTION

Ask questions to help the objector
explore his or her views in more depth.

COLLABORATE

Recognise the objection and ask the group to
include it in the session outcome/results.

When two or more participants are in conflict:

LEAD

Identify the 'correct' position and influence
the group to accept it.

INTERPERSONAL SKILLS

CONFLICT HANDLING WHEN FACILITATING DISCUSSION

When two or more participants are in conflict, help them to either:

HOLD their disagreement until later.

COMPROMISE by 'splitting the difference'.

COLLABORATE by seeking out a win/win solution.

FACILITATING DISCUSSION

CONFLICT HANDLING WHEN BRAINSTORMING/PROCESS MONITORING

When two or more participants are in conflict when **brainstorming**:

RESTATE the ground rules to which they **all** previously agreed (see page 22).

When two or more participants are in conflict when **process monitoring**:

MIRROR

Use non-judgemental reflective statements which help the whole group see what's happening and take action.

SOLUTION FINDING
TECHNIQUES

SOLUTION FINDING TECHNIQUES

1. BRAINSTORMING

When in doubt about which technique to use, you can always fall back on brainstorming! Here's a reminder of the basic rules:

- Working with a flip chart/pinboard, ask each member in turn to suggest a solution to the problem

- Record **all** ideas on the flip chart and number them to ease final selection

- Encourage and provoke participants to give ideas or pass; after two have 'passed', switch to popcorn mode where anyone can call out an idea as it comes – 'crazy' and 'stupid' ideas should be encouraged as well as those which 'piggyback' on others

- Proceed until ideas dry up, then give each participant five votes to distribute to the ideas (except their own!) in any way they wish

2. CAUSES & SOLUTIONS

'Causes and Solutions' is a tried and tested, 'safe' technique which you can use in most facilitation situations.

Once problem categories have been prioritised, break the participants into two or three smaller groups and ask each group to work on one of the problem categories.

They should brainstorm at least three root causes for this problem category (left hand side of a whiteboard or pinboard) and then at least one solution for each of these causes (right side). Make sure they 'dig deep' and look for meaningful causes.

Allow about 30 minutes for the group work and then ask each of them to present their findings in plenary or conduct a vernissage.

SOLUTION FINDING TECHNIQUES

3. CRITICAL MASS

Who are the people who must be convinced in order for change to take place?

The change becomes less daunting when people realise that you do not have to convince everyone about change – only the leaders of opinion. The rest will follow.

Ask groups to name them and report on how they plan to recruit them to the cause in plenary.

4. THIS TIME NEXT YEAR

It is now this time next year and all of our dreams have been achieved. Every business plan has been fulfilled and the mission is a reality. Now step back and describe how we did it!

What happened in between to make our dream a reality?
Use the past tense.

This technique is very useful when the group has low morale or when the barriers to change seem insurmountable.

Break into subgroups and ask each one to present their 'how we did it' story in plenary.

BUSINESS PLAN ACHIEVED

SOLUTION FINDING TECHNIQUES

5. GREENFIELD SITE

What would we do if we had no history, rules, regulations, culture or climate? If none of these things existed because we were just starting up, then how would we approach the problem?

This is a useful technique when a group is hampered by culture, habit or other restrictions.

Get small groups to imagine the consequences of these scenarios and to present their findings in plenary.

SOLUTION FINDING TECHNIQUES

6. MUST HAVE/NICE TO HAVE

In decision-making, sometimes a group becomes obsessed with democracy, allowing each suggestion to have equal weight and air time. This is why so many 'camels' are created by committees who start out trying to invent a horse.

'Must have/nice to have' is a technique to use **after** the group has surfaced a number of solutions to a problem. It gets the group to establish what key things are essential. It also allows them to place a weighting on the 'nice to have' issues, which have now become dispensable, enabling the group to move ahead with its work.

7. TIME BEAM

- Write the problem on the board and ask team members to brainstorm solutions. Each suggestion should be discussed and agreed with the team before being displayed (on cards/post-it notes)

- Get them to turn the board around and draw a diagonal line (see opposite) from top right (the deadline for problem solution) to bottom left (today's date). Ask them to rewrite each suggestion as an action step and to plot each step onto the time beam line at the appropriate 'date'

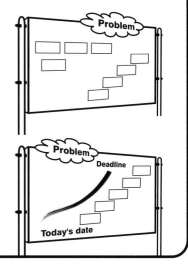

SOLUTION FINDING TECHNIQUES

8. TRANSPORTER

How would they tackle this problem in ...(Intel, HP, Volvo, Japan, USA, Malaysia?)

This is useful for abandoning traditional modes of thought or for getting free from culture for a short time.

Ask groups to work on the problem as if they were XYZ and report back in plenary.

9. PLUSES, MINUSES & INTERESTING FACTS

This technique was developed by Edward de Bono as a way of getting people to consider all aspects of a situation – the advantages, disadvantages and other incidental issues which emerge, such as new opportunities previously unseen.

It's useful if a group is fairly antagonistic to a proposal or change.

Divide the board into three sections (pluses, minuses, interesting facts) and ask three small groups each to work on one of the sections. They bring back their findings on stickies, and post them on the board/present them to the others.

SOLUTION FINDING TECHNIQUES

10. EUREKA

This is a technique for solving a problem in an illogical way by making forced associations with totally unrelated pictures.

Before posing the problem to a group, pick three pictures at random and ask them to brainstorm the first word which comes to mind. Make three lists of words and then pose the problem.

Only ideas which are generated by **combining** one word from each list may be considered and then built on and elaborated into viable solutions.

THE TALKING WALL

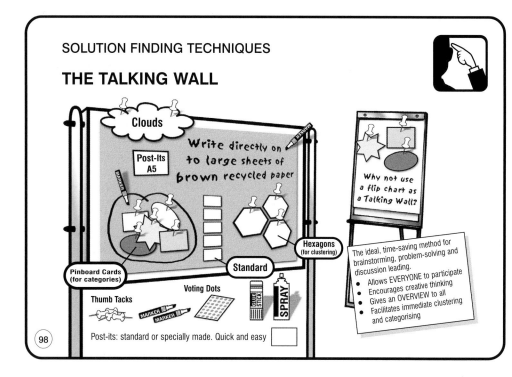

Clouds

Post-Its
A5

Write directly on to large sheets of brown recycled paper

Hexagons
(for clustering)

Pinboard Cards
(for categories)

Standard

Why not use a flip chart as a Talking Wall?

The ideal, time-saving method for brainstorming, problem-solving and discussion leading.
- Allows EVERYONE to participate
- Encourages creative thinking
- Gives an OVERVIEW to all
- Facilitates immediate clustering and categorising

Thumb Tacks

Voting Dots

GLUE STICK

SPRAY

Post-its: standard or specially made. Quick and easy

SOLUTION FINDING TECHNIQUES

VERNISSAGE

Instead of presenting the results of their group work, teams visit the Action Plan board of the other teams (like at a 'vernissage' or 'private viewing' of an exhibition at a gallery). Each participant has three possible ways of commenting **silently** on the work of his/her colleagues:

 Writing/sticking a heart shape to show agreement with any point and adding a comment which builds on that point

 Writing/sticking a 'lightning' flash to indicate disagreement with any point and adding a reason for disagreement

 Writing/sticking a question mark to say 'I don't understand this point'

You, as a facilitator, then lead the final discussion to clarify all the vernissage hearts, flashes and question marks.

SOLUTION FINDING TECHNIQUES

FORCE FIELD ANALYSIS

Force Field analysis is a powerful tool for testing the feasibility of proposed solutions to problems **before** committing to action plans. Working from the problem, write the proposed solution on the board and then divide the board into two halves.

The left side represents all the forces which are working against reaching the desired state and the right side those forces which are pushing towards reaching it. Get team members to suggest negative and positive forces. Each should be agreed with the team before being displayed (on cards/post-it notes or written directly on board) and perhaps **weighted**.

Turn the board around and make a summary of the **action steps** needed to support the positive and restrain the negative forces.

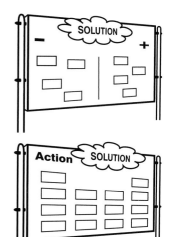

Helpful attitudes & values

MY MIND-SET WON'T HELP THEM

One of the principal errors facilitators make is that they impose their ideas on the group as they search for an answer to a particular problem. This is often because the facilitator has greater experience than the others in the group and perhaps has seen this specific situation many times in the past. The temptation is always there to try to get the group to see it your way.

In this case, the group miss out on the opportunity to discover their own way to the solution. They also lose the opportunity to discover a better way than that which is possible using the facilitator's frame of reference.

Facilitators must recognise that, in many instances, working with mature, experienced people requires that we put our own mind-sets into abeyance in order to remain neutral enough to help others.

UNCONDITIONAL POSITIVE REGARD

Facilitators draw knowledge from many other disciplines as they go about their work with groups and individuals. The counselling profession has always had a tradition of **unconditional positive regard** towards its clients, and it is an appropriate concept for facilitators' work also.

Unconditional positive regard means, briefly, that no matter what the client's personal attributes, views, appearance, behaviours, etc, the facilitator will always regard the individual as a human, unique and with enormous potential to be respected as such.

As you can imagine, this is a difficult aspiration given that so many of the people we meet can cause us discomfort, to say the least! Nevertheless, it is also vital that facilitators realise that they can't help their 'difficult' clients otherwise.

(103)

IT'S OK TO TEACH!

Some people think you should **always** facilitate; that process is **always** more important than content. Here's a modern-day parable for you to consider.

Vassili Tator is an earnest young training specialist with the United Nations in Geneva. Vassili has been taught that all human beings have unlimited potential and that the best way for people to learn is to share their knowledge with each other.

One summer Vassili set off to Papua New Guinea to teach an isolated tribe, who had survived happily for many millennia without electricity, how to use and maintain a gasoline-powered generator.

Having unpacked the crates of equipment and set up his flip charts, he gathered the scantily-clad, smiling natives around him. In well-rehearsed but halting phrases of local dialect he began:

"Now I want you to break into triads and discuss the steps you think we should take in order to complete a sound, regular maintenance of this generator. Please be ready to make a short presentation of your group's findings in 20 minutes from now."

NO ONE BEST WAY

Researchers into management behaviour have always sought the 'Holy Grail' of the one best way to manage people. More recently, however, we have come to accept that situational leadership and contingency approaches to management have real value in this diverse world. So we look for approaches which fit the situation rather than try to apply the 'one best way' to all circumstances.

There are two important lessons for facilitators here. Firstly, the principal idea behind having a facilitator work with the group is to generate a **custom-made** solution for that group and that situation. **Ready-made** solutions and answers, held by the facilitator, are probably inappropriate.

Secondly, facilitators should be open to changing the techniques and tools they themselves use when working with groups (especially when the group desires such changes). Simply adhering to the 'tried and trusted' ways of facilitating may be comfortable for the facilitator, but perhaps he or she is clinging on to tradition whilst exhorting the group to change and be flexible.

PEOPLE NEVER ARGUE WITH THEIR OWN DATA

Trainers have known this for years. Clever trainers always celebrate the data produced by the group and use it to help people to teach themselves. How many times have you seen experienced trainers post the output of group work onto the walls as 'trophies' for each group to admire? They cleverly invite experienced participants to help co-deliver parts of the course. They draw on the experience of the group in order to help them to see the value of their teaching and to prevent cognitive dissonance arising when new concepts are introduced.

It's the same for facilitators! The good ones know that the answers lie within the group and that their role is to help bring these answers out. They do this by getting the group, at all stages of the process, to understand that they own what is happening in the room and that they are the principal actors in the situation. So, every stage of the process is agreed and signed off before moving onto the next.

Before the facilitation begins, participants are encouraged to help define objectives; each individual's needs are established and recorded during the early stages of the process; participants themselves are involved in administration, such as writing up ideas and actions.

Good facilitators never get into arguments because people never argue with....

FACILITATORS CAN'T WIN ARGUMENTS

You can never win an argument with a customer! So the saying goes in good customer service texts, and the same applies in facilitation. Yet it's so tempting to engage with someone in a debate when we know exactly why and where they are wrong! If only they would just listen, see things our way, come to their senses, etc.

Skilled facilitators understand that such emotions and attitudes are counter-productive. They can empathise with someone who is being told by an 'expert' that they are wrong. They know that nobody likes being told they are wrong. Facilitators educate participants by understanding that education means 'to lead out'.

They do this by using open questions to help the challenger see the way forward: 'How would that work in practice?' 'What are the downsides to that idea?' 'What are the implications of your views?'

HELPFUL ATTITUDES & VALUES

SILENCE IS OK

In speeches and presentations a little silence can be a powerful tool for creating emphasis, or for getting audience attention. When silence lasts for longer than a few seconds in these instances, people get embarrassed. Try it yourself while chairing your next meeting and see how long it takes for someone to fill the silence with a comment or interjection, however useless it may be. We are uncomfortable with silences when it is our responsibility to present, chair or to facilitate.

Silence, however, is OK! There may be times during a facilitation when a person (or a group) has to take time to think about something important which has just happened and which needs consideration. As a facilitator your duty is to allow that to take place.

On other occasions you may have just asked a question about a sensitive issue which must be answered and dealt with by the group. Silence from you indicates that you intend to wait for the answer and that your questions are to be respected. Silence can also be used to allow an introverted group to process information internally. How much silence? Every situation is different but we would suggest that you move on after about 45 seconds!

DON'T PUSH THE RIVER

Don't push the river; it flows by itself! This is an old adage used by facilitators to indicate that you should not force a group towards a solution that they can't reach on their own.

Should facilitators pull or push? The answer seems to lie with the group.

Some facilitators will not go any further than a group wishes to initially. There are two dimensions to this. Facilitators can push a group to do more work, but they can also push a group to disclose more, and to go deeper into sensitive issues which are causing problems.

We take the view that the facilitator should push to do more work only if he/she feels there is the energy there to complete the task. In terms of disclosure and sensitive issues, the facilitator should push only as far as the group is willing to co-operate freely with the direction given.

The challenge for facilitators is that they can't push the river but they still have to make sure it gets to the sea!

NOTES

THE KNOWLEDGE BASE
Useful theories for facilitators

THE KNOWLEDGE BASE

LEARNING STYLES

Some people learn by trying something new and then thinking about it, and others by thinking first, then trying. There are four basic types of learner:

The Activist
- learns best by testing new knowledge or skills immediately and then correcting

The Reflector
- learns best by thinking carefully about how to apply new learning before acting

The Theorist
- learns best by conceptualising how the learning fits with coherent models and theories

The Pragmatist
- is highly practical; only learns if new knowledge makes sense and can help him/her achieve goals

Based on Honey & Mumford: 'Using your learning styles', 1986

THE KNOWLEDGE BASE

FOUR PHASES OF TEAM DEVELOPMENT

Form   During the start-up phase for a new team, members tentatively explore the boundaries of acceptable group behaviour. As the team forms, they want to establish themselves as participants and worry about being left out.

Storm   In the storming phase, members realise that the task is difficult and grow impatient with lack of progress. They argue about the actions the team should take, rely on their personal and professional experience, resist collaboration and become irritable and/or stubborn.

Norm   During the norming phase, members reconcile competing loyalties and responsibilities. They see the need to create rules and behavioural norms. Competitive relationships become more collaborative and the team members begin to work with each other.

Perform In the final, performing phase, team members discover each other's strengths and weaknesses, understand and accept their roles and work in synergy toward meeting their objectives.

Adapted from B.W. Tuckman: 'Developmental Sequence in Small Groups', 1965

THE KNOWLEDGE BASE

NLP

The basic premise of Neuro Linguistic Programming (NLP) is that people think about things by representing them in one of, or a mixture of, three ways:

Visually - they see pictures

Auditorily - they hear voice and sounds

Kinaesthetically - they feel emotions and sense things (touch, taste, smell)

Each person has a personal channel preference and, indeed, a personal strategy for processing information. Some of us prefer and use imagery in our speech and thoughts, others sense rather than see or hear, etc. People tend to programme themselves to think in certain ways, but this can be changed by helping them to represent things in a different way. With appropriate 'anchors' or reminders, the new ways of thinking can stick.

Trainers must be aware that participants will be processing information differently and, therefore, vary the channels on which they transmit information.

DISSONANCE & SELF-JUSTIFICATION

When we are confronted with information
which contradicts a deeply-held view,
we suffer 'cognitive dissonance'.

We have two ways of dealing with this
dissonance:

1. **Change our opinion**
2. **Self-justify**
   - discredit the source of the information
   - distort the meaning of the information
     to fit our present view
   - seek alternative evidence to support
     our present view

Based on Elliot Aronson

LOCUS OF CONTROL

The term 'locus of control' describes the way individuals attribute responsibility for events either to factors **within** themselves, or to factors **outside** their control. People who believe that control rests within themselves are referred to as **internals**. These people see themselves as being in control of their own lives. Those who believe that their lives are controlled by factors external to them, such as fate, luck and powerful people, are referred to as **externals**.

Internals are more likely to be mature, self-reliant, and responsible, to have greater levels of job satisfaction and prefer a participatory management style. Externals are less likely to be able to cope with the demands of reality. They often express unrealistic job aspirations. Internals exhibit far more self-direction and accept more responsibility for life events.

In debate, internals rely more on personal persuasion but externals use threats to win out. In choosing teams, internals are more likely to team up with those of equal or superior ability to themselves. Externals will choose people with inferior ability and delegate less.

Locus of control is a learned behaviour and it can be changed. Training programmes which bring an awareness of the current position and a knowledge of the process or mechanisms of change can be very successful.

THE KNOWLEDGE BASE

UNFREEZE, MOVE, REFREEZE

This is a very simple procedure known as **unfreeze, move and refreeze**. Yet, despite its simplicity, it is not simplistic and requires diligent application.

Kurt Lewin proposed that in a change situation it was vital to:

- **Dissolve** the crystallisation of current behaviour using a series of techniques (unfreeze)

- **Transport** to a new level of operation the entire social system (move)

- **Secure** the new system against reverting to the old ways or to some other unintended result (refreeze).

Organisations using this approach start by recognising the need for change (unfreezing); then they mobilise commitment and energy around a purpose (moving); then they institutionalise the new order (refreezing). This is only one of Lewin's many major contributions to change literature.

THE KNOWLEDGE BASE

THE BASES OF POWER

Power is the ability to influence the thoughts or actions of others. Power does not so much exist inherently in the person who has it, as in the minds of those who perceive that he has it.

French and Raven declare that power is not an entity in itself. It is the ability to influence others through five bases of power.

- **Coercive** power is exercised through punishment or threats and having control over some desired good which the other wants
- **Reward** power is being able to grant favours or benefits to someone
- **Referent** power is being attractive to another who wishes to please you
- **Expert** power is having a competence which is scarce
- **Legitimate** power is holding an office to which is attached certain rights

Informational and **connection** power have been added by recent writers to the above five bases.

ORGANISATIONAL DEVELOPMENT
A DEFINITION

"Growth can take place with or without development and vice versa. For example, a cemetery can grow without developing, so can a rubbish heap. A nation, corporation, or an individual can develop without growing ... development is an increase in capacity and potential, not an increase in attainment ... it has less to do with how much one has than with how much one can do with whatever one has."

(Ackoff, 1981)

THE KNOWLEDGE BASE

CULTURE
A DEFINITION

"Basic assumptions and beliefs
that are shared by members of an organisation, that
operate unconsciously, and that define in a basic 'taken for granted'
fashion an organisation's view of itself and its environment.
These assumptions and beliefs are learned responses to a group's
problems of internal integration. They come to be taken for granted
because they solve those problems repeatedly and reliably.
This deeper level of assumptions is to be distinguished from the
'artefacts' and 'values' that are manifestations or surface levels of
culture but not the essence of the culture."

(Schein, 1985)

THE KNOWLEDGE BASE

SELF-FULFILLING PROPHECY

Whatever we dwell on expands in our minds and becomes self-reinforcing.

If we firmly believe that others are hostile to us then we are likely to behave in an unfriendly or even an aggressive manner. People who interact with us may be entirely neutral to begin with. However, they may perceive our behaviour in a negative light. They may even consider our behaviour as an unprovoked attack. In this case, they are likely to respond in a similar vein. Instantly, our initial preconceptions will be confirmed and will have become a self-fulfilling prophecy.

The answer is to realise that our subconscious cannot take a joke. The negative self-talk which goes on inside our heads minute by minute can be changed by our command to a positive self-fulfilling prophecy.

Facilitators must remain in full control by being aware of the power of the self-fulfilling prophecy, an antidote to the negative effects of which is to be found in 'Unconditional Positive Regard' on page 103.

REFERENCES & FURTHER READING

The Action Learning Handbook: Powerful Techniques for Education, Professional Development and Training, I. McGill and A. Brockbank, RoutledgeFalmer, 2004

Corporate Learning: Proven and Practical Guidelines for Building a Sustainable Learning Strategy, M. Dilworth and F. Bordonaro, Wiley & Sons, 2005

The Handbook of Blended Learning: Global Perspectives, Local Designs, C.J. Bonk and C.R. Graham (eds), Pfeiffer, 2006

Managers Learning in Action, D. Coghlan et al. (eds), Routledge, 2004

The Strategic Use of Stories in Organisational Communication and Learning, T.L. Gargiulo, Sharpe, 2005

Learning and Development, R. Harrison, Chartered Institute of Personnel & Development, 2005

A Practical Guide to Learning in the Workplace, S.A. Malone, The Liffey Press, 2005

Psychology and Adult Learning, M. Tennant, Routledge, 2006

About the Author

John Townsend, BA MA MCIPD
John has built a reputation internationally as a leading trainer of trainers.
He is the founder of the highly-regarded Master Trainer Institute, a total
learning facility located just outside Geneva which draws trainers and
facilitators from around the world. He set up the Institute after 30 years'
experience in international consulting and human resource management
positions in the UK, France, the United States and Switzerland – notably as
European Director of Executive Development with GTE in Geneva where he had training
responsibility for over 800 managers in 15 countries. John has published a number of
management and professional guides and regularly contributes articles to leading
management and training journals.

Many thanks to Richard Bradley of the Master Trainer Institute for helping these tips and
techniques come alive in the Management courses for participants from all over the world.
You can contact Richard at: Richard@mastertrainer.ch or www.mt-institute.com

About the Author

Dr Paul Donovan
Paul is School Director of Teaching and Learning at the School
of Business, National University of Ireland Maynooth. He has
extensive management experience and has conducted a wide
range of HRD assignments in Western Europe and Asia.

Paul's professional interests include researching evaluation of
training and development interventions where he has identified
easy-to-use surrogate measures as effective replacements for
time-consuming and expensive evaluation initiatives. He has
edited seven books in a series of management texts.

Contact
To contact Paul, email paul.donovan@nuim.ie or phone 00 353 1 7086627

Your details

Name _____

Position _____

Company _____

Address _____

_____

_____

Telephone _____

Fax _____

E-mail _____

VAT No. (EC companies) _____

Your Order Ref _____

Please send me:

		No. copies
The Facilitator's	Pocketbook	☐
The _____	Pocketbook	☐
The _____	Pocketbook	☐
The _____	Pocketbook	☐

Order by Post
MANAGEMENT POCKETBOOKS LTD
LAUREL HOUSE, STATION APPROACH,
ALRESFORD, HAMPSHIRE SO24 9JH UK

Order by Phone, Fax or Internet
Telephone: +44 (0)1962 735573
Facsimile: +44 (0)1962 733637
Email: sales@pocketbook.co.uk
Web: www.pocketbook.co.uk

Customers in USA should contact:
Management Pocketbooks
2427 Bond Street, University Park, IL 60466
Telephone: 866 620 6944 Facsimile: 708 534 7803
Email: mp.orders@ware-pak.com
Web: www.managementpocketbooks.com

**Other titles by John Townsend and Paul Donovan
in the Pocketbook series**

The Pocketfiles

Inspire, inform and integrate your team with these three imaginative and creative Pocketfiles – the work of the inspirational trainer John Townsend. Participants will learn key management skills in a lively and entertaining manner.

Pocketbooks – *available in both paperback and digital formats*

360 Degree Feedback*
Absence Management
Appraisals
Assertiveness
Balance Sheet
Body Language
Business Planning
Career Transition
Coaching
Cognitive Behavioural Coaching
Communicator's
Competencies
Confidence
Creative Manager's
C.R.M.
Cross-cultural Business
Customer Service
Decision-making
Delegation
Developing People
Discipline & Grievance
Diversity*
Emotional Intelligence
Employment Law
Empowerment*
Energy and Well-being
Facilitator's
Feedback

Flexible Working*
Handling Complaints
Handling Resistance
Icebreakers
Impact & Presence
Improving Efficiency
Improving Profitability
Induction
Influencing
Interviewer's
I.T. Trainer's
Key Account Manager's
Leadership
Learner's
Management Models
Manager's
Managing Assessment Centres
Managing Budgets
Managing Cashflow
Managing Change
Managing Customer Service
Managing Difficult Participants
Managing Recruitment
Managing Upwards
Managing Your Appraisal
Marketing
Meetings
Memory

Mentoring
Motivation
Negotiator's
Networking
NLP
Nurturing Innovation
Openers & Closers
People Manager's
Performance Management
Personal Success
Positive Mental Attitude
Presentations
Problem Behaviour
Project Management
Psychometric Testing
Resolving Conflict
Reward
Sales Excellence
Salesperson's
Self-managed Development
Starting In Management
Storytelling
Strategy
Stress
Succeeding at Interviews
Sustainability
Tackling Difficult Conversations
Talent Management

Teambuilding Activities
Teamworking
Telephone Skills
Telesales*
Thinker's
Time Management
Trainer's
Training Evaluation
Training Needs Analysis
Transfer of Learning
Virtual Teams
Vocal Skills
Working Relationships
Workplace Politics
Writing Skills

* only available as an e-book

Pocketfiles

Trainer's Blue Pocketfile of
Ready-to-use Activities

Trainer's Green Pocketfile of
Ready-to-use Activities

Trainer's Red Pocketfile of
Ready-to-use Activities

To order please visit us at **www.pocketbook.co.uk**

03.01.14